DATING & HANGING OUT

BY Will Eisner

SCHOLASTIC INC.
New York Toronto London Auckland Sydney

No part of this publication may be reproduced in whole or in part, or stored in a retrieval system, or transmitted in any form or by any means, electronic, mechanical, photocopying, recording, or otherwise, without written permission of the publisher. For information regarding permission, write to Scholastic Inc., 730 Broadway, New York, NY 10003.

ISBN 0-590-30031-8

Copyright © 1979 by Will Eisner. All Rights Reserved. This edition is published by Scholastic Inc., by arrangement with Poorhouse Press.

12 11 10 9 8 7 6 5 4   0 1 2/9

Printed in the U.S.A.   01

This Book is About...
Dating, Going Steady, Coming On, & Hanging Out

IT IS A GLEEFUL GUIDE TO PERSONAL RELATIONSHIPS AND CONTAINS ALMOST EVERYTHING YOU NEED TO KNOW.

DATING IS A SOCIAL ACTIVITY
IN WHICH TWO PEOPLE JOIN TO SHARE AN EXPERIENCE

IN THE BEGINNING ...
WHEN PEOPLE WANTED TO SHARE
AN EXPERIENCE WITH SOMEONE, THEY
SIMPLY WENT OUT AND GRABBED
THE FIRST AVAILABLE PERSON.
IT WAS AN ERA OF
INSTANT DATING.

THEN, SOMEONE INVENTED SIGNAL DRUMS—WHICH CHANGED EVERYTHING! DATING WAS NO LONGER AD-LIB! FOR ONE THING, IT REQUIRED CONSENT.

IT WAS OBVIOUS DATING HAD TO BE APPROACHED MORE SCIENTIFICALLY. THE EARLY EGYPTIANS DECIDED TO TRY COSMETICS, WHICH THEY HOPED WOULD ATTRACT PEOPLE TO EACH OTHER WITHOUT PRELIMINARY NEGOTIATION. IT DIDN'T ALWAYS WORK OUT!

IN RECENT YEARS, A LONELY SCIENTIST, WHO WAS PERPETUALLY REJECTED BY GIRLS NOTICED THAT ANIMALS WERE ATTRACTED TO EACH OTHER WITHOUT THE USE OF TELEPHONES OR DISCOS. HE ALSO DISCOVERED THAT ANIMALS SECRETE A CHEMICAL CALLED PHEREMONES—THE ODOR OF WHICH CAN CREATE INSTANT SOCIAL RELATIONSHIPS.

SO, HE DISTILLED A BATCH OF THE PHEREMONE EXTRACT, DOUSED HIMSELF AND WAITED FOR THE ANIMAL MAGNETISM TO BEGIN.

UNFORTUNATELY, NOTHING HAPPENED!

HE WAITED BY THE PHONE FOR FORTY YEARS ... IT NEVER EVEN RANG ONCE. GIRLS AVOIDED HIM! HE WAS, HOWEVER, VERY, VERY ATTRACTIVE TO DOGS ... AND WHEN THEY FOUND HIM, DEAD AT AGE 91, THERE WERE 400 ANIMALS IN HIS HOUSE.

THE RULES OF SUCCESSFUL DATING

SINCE A DEPENDENCE ON CHEMISTRY ALONE IS NOT ENOUGH, SUCCESSFUL DATING MUST BE APPROACHED SCIENTIFICALLY.
SCIENCE TELLS US THAT HUMAN CONDUCT IS MEASURABLE AND THE BEHAVIORAL SCIENTISTS RECOGNIZE THAT ONCE SUCH PATTERNS ARE FULLY UNDERSTOOD BEHAVIOR MODIFICATION CAN BE EMPLOYED.
ACTUALLY, ALL THIS JARGON MEANS IS ...
IN DATING, YOU DEAL WITH THE USUAL RULES OF LIVING.

DATING IS SUBJECT TO THE LAW OF SUPPLY & DEMAND

HOW TO KNOW IF YOU ARE SHY

YOU KNOW YOU **ARE** SHY IF...
YOU PREFER TO LOOK AT THE PICTURES ON THE WALL RATHER THAN TALK TO THE OTHERS AT SOCIAL GATHERINGS.

(ASSUMING, OF COURSE, THAT THE CROWD ISN'T A BUNCH OF CREEPS OR YOU HAVE BAD BREATH.)

THE MERE MENTION OF YOUR NAME (EVEN AFTER YOU HAVE CHANGED IT TWICE) CAUSES YOU TO BLUSH!

HI, GWENHULDA, WHAT'S NEW?

YOU KNOW YOU ARE SHY...

WHEN YOU GO TO HANG UP YOUR COAT IN THE CLOSET AT A PARTY AND....
YOU STAY THERE!

YOU ENJOY SUBWAY RUSH HOURS....
BECAUSE YOU CAN HIDE EASILY.

OVERCOMING SHYNESS

ACTUALLY, THE RESISTANCE YOU FEAR MOST IS ILLUSORY. SO, THE TRICK IS TO MAKE YOURSELF INSTANTLY ACCEPTABLE WITHOUT HAVING TO ALTER YOUR INHIBITIONS, WHICH MAY BE HOPELESSLY DEEP-ROOTED.

TALK LOUD! IT DOESN'T MATTER IF WHAT YOU SAY IS DUMB. PEOPLE WILL THINK IT'S IMPORTANT AND WILL IMMEDIATELY RESPOND. YOU CAN RETREAT BACK INTO YOUR SHELL WHILE THEY DO ALL THE TALKING.

GET A FRIEND TO ASK YOUR OPINION WHEN IN A GROUP SITUATION. OR IF YOU HATE TO TALK, ASK THEM TO QUOTE YOU.

WEAR SHADES. YOU CAN HIDE BEHIND THEM. TRY MIRROR GLASSES. THIS BRINGS PEOPLE UP CLOSE AND CAN LEAD TO AN EASY OPENING.

VERY DARK SHADES ARE GREAT FOR OVERCOMING SHYNESS BECAUSE YOU CAN ALWAYS PRETEND YOU HADN'T NOTICED

START AN OUTRAGEOUS RUMOR ABOUT YOURSELF. PEOPLE WILL WANT TO MEET YOU. THEY WILL MAKE THE FIRST MOVE, SPARING YOU THE AGONY OF STARTING A CONVERSATION.

THE BEAUTY OF THIS PLOY IS THAT YOU DON'T EVEN HAVE TO TALK AT ALL IF YOU DON'T WANT TO.

CHOOSING DATES

HERE IS A HANDY GUIDE TO SELECTING PEOPLE. KEEP IN MIND YOUR OWN PERSONALITY TRAITS.

THE QUIET, INTROSPECTIVE TYPE

THESE PEOPLE GENERALLY DO WELL WITH THE OUTGOING TYPE OF PERSON. THEY NEED A PARTNER WHO WILL DO ALL THE WORK NECESSARY TO GENERATE EXCITEMENT. THEY DON'T LIKE TO BE THE FIRST TO DO ANYTHING. ALSO, THEY RARELY HAVE ANY IDEAS ABOUT WHAT THEY WANT TO DO OR WHERE TO GO.

THE OUTGOING TYPE

THESE PEOPLE ARE ALWAYS IN ACTION. THEY GO WHERE THE ACTION IS. THEY'LL TRY ANYTHING. THEY HAVE LOTS OF ENERGY AND MAKE THINGS HAPPEN. THE TROUBLE IS IT USUALLY HAPPENS TO THE QUIET PERSON THEY LIKE TO DATE. THEY'RE ALSO PRETTY FICKLE.

 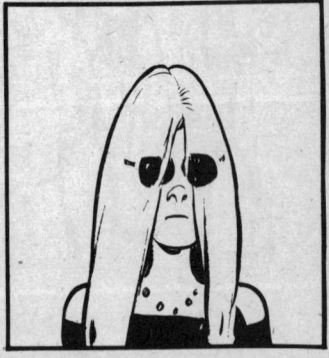

THE FREAKED OUT TYPE

THESE PEOPLE DO NOT CARE . . . THAT IS, THEY'RE NOT TOO PARTICULAR ABOUT WHO THEY DATE. THEY ARE SO OUT OF IT THAT THEY DON'T KNOW WHO THEY DATE. YOU MIGHT SET THEM UP WITH YOUR COUSIN WHO CAN'T FIND A DATE.

VERY OFTEN THE CHOICE OF A DATE PARTNER CAN BE A CHALLENGE. WHO KNOWS, PERHAPS YOU CAN BE THE ONE TO ALTER SOMEONE'S SOCIAL OUTLOOK.

THE GLAMOUR TYPE
THESE PEOPLE LIVE IN A WORLD THAT'S BUILT AROUND THEMSELVES. THEY'RE BEAUTIFUL AND KNOW IT. THEY EXPECT YOU TO BE GRATEFUL FOR THEM. USE THEM TO HELP YOU GET EVEN OR "EAT-THE-HEART" OUT OF THAT AWFUL PERSON WHO HAS DROPPED YOU FOR SOMEONE ELSE.

SPECIAL BREEDS
THESE PEOPLE ARE HARD TO GET INVOLVED WITH. THEY DO THEIR THING, PERIOD. IF WHAT THEY DO IS ALSO YOUR BAG, GREAT . . . OTHERWISE DON'T WASTE YOUR TIME.

THE INTELLECTUALS
THESE PEOPLE ARE NOT EASY TO HANG OUT WITH. THEY ARE NOT CONCERNED WITH THE IMPORTANT THINGS LIKE . . . WHAT TRAVOLTA'S LATEST OFF-SCREEN ROMANCE IS DOING TO HIS CAREER. BUT YOUR PARENTS WILL LOVE THEM.

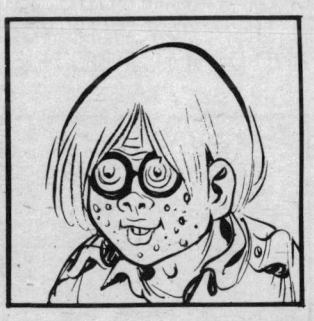

THE HOBBYISTS
THEY ARE INTO COLLECTING COMICS, PLAYING THE SITAR, TRIBAL DANCES, COMPUTER MUSIC, ASTRONOMY, DOLL HOUSES, AND MINIATURE TRAINS. THEY ARE TOO BUSY TO APPRECIATE THE FUN OF DOING NOTHING. THEY ARE GREAT FOR KNOWING ABOUT FREE LECTURES.

THE IDEAL TYPES

THESE PEOPLE ARE FANTASTIC. THEY'RE VERY NICE, THEY ARE PRETTY; THEY ARE INTERESTING. THEY ENJOY DOING FUN THINGS, THEY ARE POPULAR AND GET INVITED TO THE BEST PARTIES. THEY ARE ABSOLUTELY COOL. THE TROUBLE IS WHY SHOULD THEY WASTE THEIR TIME WITH **YOU**? FRANKLY, THEY CAN . . . AND DO A LOT BETTER.

CREEPS

DON'T OVERLOOK THEM. THEY MAY BE, UGH, GROSS, BUT THEY USUALLY HAVE TERRIFIC FRIENDS OR COUSINS WHO YOU CAN ONLY MEET THROUGH THEM. ALSO PEOPLE WILL PITY YOU AND INTRODUCE YOU TO SOMEONE BETTER.

LEARN TO IGNORE PEER PRESSURE

OBVIOUSLY YOUR FRIENDS' OPINIONS WILL HAVE AN INFLUENCE . . . BUT, REMEMBER THAT IT IS **YOUR** TASTE IN PEOPLE THAT COUNTS.

USING ASTROLOGY AS A GUIDE TO SELECTING A DATE

ASTROLOGY IS A KIND OF CULT-SCIENCE
WHICH CLAIMS THAT HUMAN PERSONALITY
IS INFLUENCED BY THE DATE OF BIRTH.
IN THIS WAY THE COMPATABILITY OF TWO
PEOPLE CAN OFTEN BE PREDICTED.
EACH MONTH OF THE YEAR HAS A **SIGN**
WHICH SERVES TO IDENTIFY THE TYPE.
PEOPLE BORN UNDER THESE SIGNS
HAVE CERTAIN CHARACTERISTICS. KNOWING
WHAT THESE ARE IS ONE BASIS OF YOUR
JUDGMENT OF THEM AS A DATE.

UPON MEETING A NEW PERSON WHO
YOU THINK MIGHT BE A POTENTIAL DATE,
EXCHANGE SUN SIGNS. NOT ONLY DOES
IT MAKE A GOOD OPENING LINE . . . BUT
IT COULD PRODUCE SOME AMAZING RESULTS.

ARIES

BIRTH DATE: MARCH 21—APRIL 19

THESE PEOPLE ARE EASILY IDENTIFIED BY THEIR NEAT APPEARANCE AND SLIM PHYSIQUES. THEY OFTEN PREFER BRIGHT RED CLOTHING AND A SIMPLICITY IN STYLE. THIS IS BECAUSE THEY ARE ENERGETIC AND UNCOMPLICATED. GENERALLY THEY . . . "WANT TO DO SOMETHING IMMEDIATELY." THEY LIKE ACTION, OFTEN WITHOUT THINKING OF THE CONSEQUENCES. THEY ARE LEADERS BY INSTINCT AND HAVE HUGE EGOS.

ARIES GIRLS ARE ATTRACTED TO JUDO WHILE BOYS LIKE LOUD MUSIC.

ARIES PEOPLE USUALLY HAVE ARCHED EYEBROWS.

ARIES MOTHERS TEND TO LOOK LIKE RAMS IN LATER YEARS.

INSTANT REFERENCE TO DATING WITH A ARIES

IF YOU ARE ONE OF THESE	GOING STEADY	HANGING OUT
ARIES	Mayhem!!	Casual
TAURUS	Trouble!	Embarrassing
GEMINI	Uphill!	Good fun
CANCER	Good!!	Off-and-on
LEO	Competitive!!	Conflicts
VIRGO	Nagging	Not smooth
LIBRA	Great!!	Excellent
SCORPIO	Avoid it!!	Fights
SAGITTARIUS	Bickering	Good!
CAPRICORN	Busy!!	Nope!!
AQUARIUS	Splendid!	Great
PISCES	Nah!!	Patience, pal!!

TAURUS

BIRTH DATE: APRIL 20—MAY 20

THE TAURUS PERSONS ARE CONSERVATIVE IN THEIR CLOTHING. THEY HAVE A TENDENCY TO THICK NECKS, LOW FOREHEADS, AND CURLY HAIR. THEY HAVE A TOWERING RAGE IN AN ARGUMENT AND LOVE TO EAT SWEETS. THEY PREFER WARM CLIMATES, AND GAIN WEIGHT EASILY.

TAURUS PEOPLE HAVE TROUBLE MAKING UP THEIR MINDS.

INSTANT REFERENCE TO DATING WITH A TAURUS

IF YOU ARE ONE OF THESE	GOING STEADY	HANGING OUT
ARIES	Okay!	Dull
TAURUS	Good deal	Envy & Jealousy
GEMINI	Boring	No conversation
CANCER	Secure	Yep!!
LEO	Dangerous	Won't last
VIRGO	Yes	Hard work
LIBRA	"Iffy"	Smooth!
SCORPIO	Dull	You'll be #2
SAGITTARIUS	Too hectic	No way!
CAPRICORN	Arguments	Enduring
AQUARIUS	No!!	Too rough
PISCES	Fine . . .	Not bad!

GEMINI

BIRTH DATE: MAY 21—JUNE 21

GEMINI PEOPLE HAVE A RATHER BOUNCY STYLE OF WALK. THEY'RE ALWAYS "ON-THE-GO" THEY ARE USUALLY SMALL AND SLIM. THEY GIVE OFF GREAT NERVOUS VIBES. THEY'LL OFTEN DO SEVERAL PROJECTS AT THE SAME TIME.

GEMINIS WALK WITH AN UP AND DOWN STEP

GEMINI STUDENTS LIKE TO DO THEIR HOMEWORK WHILE WATCHING T V

GEMINIS ARE VERY GOOD AT PING PONG

GEMINIS MAKE GOOD FOOTBALL SCRAMBLERS

INSTANT REFERENCE TO DATING WITH A GEMINI

IF YOU ARE ONE OF THESE	GOING STEADY	HANGING OUT
ARIES	Great	Great
TAURUS	Ha, ha, ha!	Boring
GEMINI	Why not?	Lots of talk
CANCER	Won't work!	Avoid it
LEO	Wear ear plugs	Good luck!
VIRGO	Odd-couple	A talk-a-thon!
LIBRA	Lively	Compatible
SCORPIO	Too busy!!	Gossipy
SAGITTARIUS	Fine!	Sensational
CAPRICORN	If you're firm	Don't bother
AQUARIUS	Fragile	Life-long
PISCES	Temporary	Off-and-on

CANCER

BIRTH DATE: JUNE 22—JULY 21

IT'S HARD TO IDENTIFY A CANCER PERSON BY SHAPE OR SIZE, THEY VARY SO. BUT THEY WORRY A LOT ABOUT THEMSELVES. THEIR FACES ARE SOMEWHAT FLAT. AND THEIR COMPLEXIONS ARE OFTEN PALE. MOSTLY CANCER PEOPLE HAVE A FURROW BETWEEN THEIR EYEBROWS. THEY ARE SENTIMENTAL.

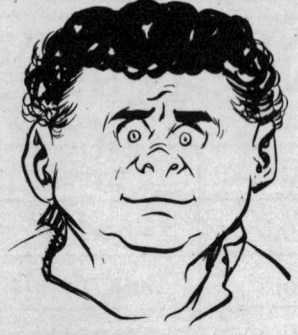 

THEY ARE NOT VERY INTERESTED IN CLOTHES OR STYLE. THEY NEVER THROW OLD CLOTHES AWAY.

IT'LL COME BACK IN FASHION ANY DAY NOW!

CANCERIANS MAKE GOOD BOY SCOUTS.

INSTANT REFERENCE TO DATING WITH A CANCER

IF YOU ARE ONE OF THESE	GOING STEADY	HANGING OUT
ARIES	Yes	Boring
TAURUS	Solid!	Steady
GEMINI	Emotional	Fleeting
CANCER	A drag	Solid!
LEO	Forget it!	Slow
VIRGO	No!	Ideal!!
LIBRA	One-sided!	You'll get hurt!
SCORPIO	Fights!!	Exciting
SAGITTARIUS	Don't!!	A drag
CAPRICORN	Okay!	It's your ball
AQUARIUS	Won't last!	No!
PISCES	Snug!	Be careful

LEO

BIRTH DATE: JULY 22—AUGUST 21

THESE PEOPLE ARE BIG SHOW OFFS. THEY LIKE JAZZY CLOTHES. THEY GENERALLY HAVE LONG NOSES AND HAVE A WEIGHT PROBLEM. THEY HAVE STRAIGHT BACKS, SMALL WAISTS, AND SHORT LEGS.

INSTANT REFERENCE TO DATING WITH A LEO

IF YOU ARE ONE OF THESE	GOING STEADY	HANGING OUT
ARIES	They dominate	Bickering
TAURUS	A fight!	Go easy!
GEMINI	Excellent	Steady
CANCER	Don't try!!	Okay!
LEO	Great	A scramble
VIRGO	Nah!!	Fine
LIBRA	Poverty!!	Expensive
SCORPIO	Rocky	Jumping
SAGITTARIUS	Why not?	Simpatico!
CAPRICORN	Careful!!	Cloying
AQUARIUS	Yes!	No way!
PISCES	Fabulous	Arm's length

VIRGO

BIRTH DATE: AUGUST 22—SEPT. 22

VIRGO PEOPLE ARE RESTLESS. DATING THEM WILL MEAN YOU WILL HAVE TO WORK HARD TO KEEP THEM AMUSED. THEY DO NOT LIKE LONG ABSTRACT CONVERSATIONS OR SOUL SEARCHING SESSIONS. THEY ARE USUALLY THE HARDEST WORKING PEOPLE IN THE CLUB.

THEY USUALLY HAVE A "WIDOWS PEAK" HAIRLINE. THEY HAVE WILLOWY FIGURES AND ARE QUICK OF MOVEMENT.

INSTANT REFERENCE TO DATING WITH A VIRGO

IF YOU ARE ONE OF THESE	GOING STEADY	HANGING OUT
ARIES	So, so!	Hectic
TAURUS	Good	Whew!
GEMINI	Abrasive	Fun
CANCER	Maybe!	Happy times
LEO	No way!	It's work!
VIRGO	Bickering	You'll like it!
LIBRA	Too busy!	Won't last
SCORPIO	Good	Enjoy it!
SAGITTARIUS	Nag, nag, nag!	Carping
CAPRICORN	Excellent	Very sound
AQUARIUS	Stable	Good!!
PISCES	Okay!	Avoid it!

LIBRA

BIRTH DATE: SEPTEMBER 23 — OCT. 22

LIBRA PEOPLE ARE GENERALLY RELAXED IN THEIR MANNER. THEY ALWAYS SEEM TO BE UNCOMPLICATED IN THEIR LIFE STYLE. THEY ARE ORDERLY IN MOST EVERYTHING THEY DO. LIBRAS ARE ALSO QUITE ROMANTIC AND LIKE MOVIES THAT INVOLVE LOVE STORIES OR HISTORICAL ADVENTURES. THE BOYS LIKE COOL BLUE COLORS AND THE GIRLS LIKE LOOSE FITTING CLOTHES. STRANGELY, THEY TEND TO COCK THEIR HEAD TO A SIDE DURING A CONVERSATION.

INSTANT REFERENCE TO DATING WITH A LIBRA

IF YOU ARE ONE OF THESE	GOING STEADY	HANGING OUT
ARIES	Fine!	Avoid it
TAURUS	Yes	Great
GEMINI	Romantic	Fun
CANCER	Quibbling	Careful
LEO	You're boss	Enjoy!!
VIRGO	Maybe	A drag
LIBRA	Excellent	Swinging!
SCORPIO	If you're alert	Interesting
SAGITTARIUS	Milk 'n' honey	Patience
CAPRICORN	Marvelous!	You'll like it!
AQUARIUS	Fun . . . but!!!	Fine!
PISCES	A good fit	Go easy!

SCORPIO

BIRTH DATE: OCTOBER 23—NOVEMBER 21

SCORPIO PEOPLE ARE INTENSE. IN GATHERINGS THEY USUALLY STAND OUT. THEY HAVE A TENDENCY TO GET INTO ARGUMENTS. THEY OFTEN BROWBEAT PEOPLE THEY THINK ARE LESS INTELLIGENT THAN THEY ARE. THEY KNOW ALL ABOUT **THEIR** FAVORITE SINGERS OR MUSIC GROUPS. THEY THINK ANYBODY ELSE'S CHOICE IS AWFUL. THEY ARE AT THE SAME TIME FASCINATING PEOPLE. THEY LIKE TO WEAR VERY DARK LEATHER CLOTHES AND HAVE AN AIR OF MYSTERY ABOUT THEM. THEY HAVE A DARK-EYED LOOK!

Instant Reference to Dating with a Scorpio

If you are one of these	Going Steady	Hanging Out
Aries	Mayhem!!	Scrappy!
Taurus	Heh, heh, yes!	Stable
Gemini	Hard work	Good
Cancer	You'll get hurt!	So, so
Leo	Boom!!	A scrimmage
Virgo	Bickering	Great
Libra	Won't last	Fast
Scorpio	Good!	Arguments
Sagittarius	A jail term!	Not easy
Capricorn	Not bad!	Good!
Aquarius	Forget it!	Brittle
Pisces	Yes!	Try hard!

SAGITTARIUS

BIRTH DATE: NOVEMBER 22—DECEMBER 21

SAGITTARIANS ARE A LIVELY LOT. THEY HAVE AN OPEN, HUMOROUS OUTLOOK. THEY ARE VERY OPEN ABOUT THEMSELVES AND ARE GENERALLY CANDID. THEY ATTRACT PEOPLE WITH THEIR OUTGOING STYLE. THEY ARE GREAT SPORTS PEOPLE AND KEEP THEMSELVES IN CONDITION.

THEY HAVE WIDE FOREHEADS AND STRAIGHT EYEBROWS. THEY ARE VORACIOUS EATERS. THE BOYS HATE TO WEAR TIES AND THE GIRLS FAVOR PURPLE SCARVES. THEY PREFER DATES THAT INCLUDE SOME ATHLETIC ACTIVITIES.

INSTANT REFERENCE TO DATING WITH A SAGITTARIUS

IF YOU ARE ONE OF THESE	GOING STEADY	HANGING OUT
ARIES	Casual	Exciting
TAURUS	Hard to hold	Uphill
GEMINI	Good	Ideal
CANCER	Clashes!	Forget it
LEO	All right	Lively
VIRGO	Fine	Compatible
LIBRA	Okay!	Take over!
SCORPIO	Risky!!	On-and-off
SAGITTARIUS	"Iffy"	Outdoors
CAPRICORN	Uphill!	Too casual
AQUARIUS	Good	Excellent
PISCES	"Iffy"	Yes, sure!

CAPRICORN

BIRTH DATE: DECEMBER 22—JANUARY 20

A PLEASANT BUT LOW-KEY LOT. THEY SEEM MORE SHY THAN OTHERS BECAUSE THEY AVOID **"MAKING WAVES."** THEY DON'T LIKE TO ATTRACT ATTENTION TO THEMSELVES. THEY DRESS IN **"QUIET"** CLOTHES. AT SCHOOL THEY ARE THE ONES WHO ARE THE STEADY WORKERS. THEY HATE HOT WEATHER AND DON'T BUNDLE UP MUCH IN COLD CLIMATES CAPRICORNS SEEM TO BE ABLE TO SMILE WHILE FROWNING DUE TO THEIR **"CHEEK CREASE."** ON A DATE THEY'LL LET YOU DO THE TALKING AND WILL NOT ARGUE MUCH.

INSTANT REFERENCE TO DATING WITH A CAPRICORN

IF YOU ARE ONE OF THESE	GOING STEADY	HANGING OUT
ARIES	Conventional	Nip-and-tuck
TAURUS	Solid	Pals!!
GEMINI	Rocky!	Avoid it!
CANCER	Tense!	Interesting
LEO	Okay, if . . .	Not bad
VIRGO	Yawn!	Good!
LIBRA	Great	They lead
SCORPIO	Sparks	"Iffy"
SAGITTARIUS	Confining	Fun
CAPRICORN	Good!!	It'll be nice
AQUARIUS	Solid	A bit slow
PISCES	Good	Avoid it!!

AQUARIUS

BIRTH DATE: JANUARY 21—FEBRUARY 19

AQUARIANS ARE A VERY ATTRACTIVE PEOPLE. AT GATHERINGS THEY ARE USUALLY THE CENTER OF THINGS. THEY SPEAK FRANKLY AND HAVE CLEAR IDEAS ABOUT THINGS. THEY ARE QUITE INDEPENDENT, OFTEN HAVE UNORTHODOX IDEAS, AND STIR UP CONTROVERSY WHICH THEY ENJOY. AT SCHOOL THEY USUALLY JOIN OFF-BEAT CLUBS AND TAKE UNUSUAL SUBJECTS. THEY HAVE AN ADVENTUROUS NATURE. AQUARIANS WILL GENERALLY JOIN PROTEST GROUPS AND LIKE TO DEFEND THE UNDERDOG. ON DATES THEY LIKE TO DO INTERESTING THINGS. THEY LIKE THE LATEST STYLES IN CLOTHES AND SEEM TALLER THAN THE PEOPLE THEY HANG OUT WITH.

— STRANGE, YOU SAY *I'M* TALL — I'M THE SHORTEST ONE ON THE BASKETBALL TEAM!

WELL, IT'S ODD YOU WOULD THINK *I'M* SHORT — I'M THE TALLEST ONE ON THE HOCKEY TEAM!

Instant Reference to Dating with a Aquarius

IF YOU ARE ONE OF THESE	GOING STEADY	HANGING OUT
ARIES	Forget it!!	Fine!
TAURUS	Nah!	Fast
GEMINI	Pretty good	Arguments
CANCER	...EEH!!	Conversational
LEO	Great	No sweat
VIRGO	Fooey!	Intellectual
LIBRA	Okay	They dominate
SCORPIO	No way	Off-and-on
SAGITTARIUS	Lotsa luck	Smooth
CAPRICORN	Solid but dull	Enduring
AQUARIUS	Good	Mutual
PISCES	Tough	Maybe

PISCES

BIRTH DATE: FEBRUARY 20—MARCH 20

PISCES PEOPLE ARE VERY CREATIVE AS A RULE. THEY ARE GOOD AT AND ARE USUALLY INVOLVED IN ART. IF THEY CAN'T PARTICIPATE THEY LIKE TO BE AROUND ART. THEY WORRY A LOT. THEY ARE BIG ON THE GUILT TRIP, BUT THEY STILL TAKE CHANCES. THEY ARE VERY WILLING TO ENJOY THINGS AND ARE QUITE ROMANTIC IN THEIR OUTLOOK. THEY FALL IN LOVE OFTEN. AS A DATE YOU WILL OFTEN WIND UP WAITING FOR THEM BECAUSE THEY ARE NOT TOO PUNCTUAL. BUT YOU'LL FORGIVE THEM BECAUSE THEY ARE LIKEABLE. THEY WORRY ABOUT THEIR FEET . . . LIKE TO BUY NEW SHOES BUT WEAR THEIR OLD ONES.

A PISCES EYES ARE USUALLY QUITE SOULFUL.

PISCES PEOPLE WEAR EITHER VERY NEAT OR VERY SLOPPY FOOTWEAR.

Instant Reference to Dating with a Pisces

IF YOU ARE ONE OF THESE	GOING STEADY	HANGING OUT
ARIES	Hard work	Too slow!!
TAURUS	Great!!	Smooth
GEMINI	Could be!	Dependable
CANCER	Romantic	Nice!
LEO	Good!!	Sensational
VIRGO	So, so	Tough, but . . .
LIBRA	Okay, but . . .	Dull
SCORPIO	Forget it!	Exciting
SAGITTARIUS	Sure!!	Travel?—Yes!
CAPRICORN	Okay!!	Dull
AQUARIUS	Ho, hum	Intellectual
PISCES	A standoff!!	Yawn!!

YOU CAN FIND GIRLS AT AMUSEMENT PARKS

PEOPLE LOVE TO GO ON SCARY RIDES AND SCREAM. THERE IS A GOOD CHANCE SOME GIRL WILL HANG ONTO THE NEAREST PERSON FOR SAFETY (YOU) ... TRY NOT TO SHOW HOW SCARED YOU ARE.

WHERE TO FIND BOYS

BOYS HANG AROUND WATER COOLERS... THEY ARE A VERY THIRSTY GROUP.

MOVE TO A STATE WHERE BOYS OUTNUMBER GIRLS

OVERALL—FEMALES OUTNUMBER MALES IN THE UNITED STATES! BUT... THERE ARE THREE STATES WHERE MALES OUTNUMBER THE FEMALES.

THEY ARE:

NEVADA
248,000 MALES
vs.
241,000 FEMALES

•

ALASKA
163,000 MALES
vs.
137,000 FEMALES

•

HAWAII
399,000 MALES
vs.
369,000 FEMALES

COMING ON

MOVE IN CAREFULLY TO AVOID EMBARRASSMENT.

FANTASTIC OPENING LINES

*(NOTE) WHAT TO DO IF IT GETS TOO DEEP.

BE INVENTIVE...

INSTANT GRABBERS

FOR CROWDED PARTIES

YOUR PERSONAL IMAGE

MOST PEOPLE THINK IN STEREOTYPES. THEY ARE INFLUENCED BY MOVIES AND TV. THE INTEREST YOU GENERATE, THEREFORE, STARTS WITH WHAT YOU LOOK LIKE.

FOR EXAMPLE:

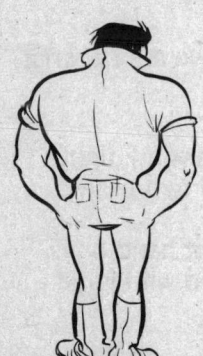

MACHO TYPES SEEM TO ATTRACT WEAK, MOUSY PEOPLE.

SOPHISTICATED WOMEN OFTEN ATTRACT RATHER SHY AND CONSERVATIVE TYPES.

SOPHISTICATED

DON'T SHOW MUCH EMOTION. IF YOUR DATE TELLS A JOKE GIVE HIM A BRIFF SMILE OF APPRECIATION . . . NOTHING MORE.

LET HIM OPEN DOORS FOR YOU. WAIT UNTIL HE DOES SO IF HE'S FORGETFUL.

How to be Macho 1

- Wear shades
- Look cool, bored, mean.
- Chew a toothpick.
- Paste a hairpiece on your chest.
- Wear a scary medallion.
- Wear an iron belt and chain.
- Wear leather wristlets.
- Keep pumping iron.
- Wear leather pants.
- Don't wear socks.
- Wear cowboy boots with spurs.

MACHO

OPEN POP BOTTLES WITH YOUR TEETH

SLUMP!... NEVER SIT OR WALK UPRIGHT ... ALWAYS LOOK BORED, ANGRY OR SLEEPY!

"DON'T YOU THINK THIS MOVIE SAYS IT ALL? — LIKE, I MEAN... IT EXPRESSES A WHOLE GAMUT OF EMOTIONS!"

"YUP!"

LET YOUR GIRL DO THE TALKING. NEVER USE A SENTENCE WITH MORE THAN ONE WORD.

BEING COOL

WHEN MEETING FOR A DATE . . . ON A
STREET CORNER—OR AT A RESTAURANT—
DON'T BE THE FIRST TO ARRIVE.

THE BLIND DATE

HOW TO DATE A ROCK STAR

THINK ROCK! LEARN HIS BEAT! DO EVERYTHING IN TIME TO HIS MUSIC.

FOR A WHOLE WEEK BEFORE THE DATE, LISTEN TO ALL HIS MUSIC. LEARN THE WORDS.

WHEN YOU SHOW UP BE COOL—WEAR SHADES. FAINT AT THE SIGHT OF HIM.

WHEN DATING A ROCK STAR MAKE SURE HE KNOWS YOU HATE EVERY OTHER ROCK STAR BUT HIM. BE LOYAL!!

WHEN HE IS BESIEGED BY FANS. STAY CLOSE TO HIM. THEY'LL PROBABLY MISTAKE YOU FOR SOMEONE FAMOUS TOO.

GET A LOCK OF HIS HAIR . . . THIS WILL PROVE TO YOUR FRIENDS THAT YOU REALLY DID DATE HIM.

HOW TO DATE A MOVIE STAR

BRUSH YOUR TEETH, USE MOUTH WASH. COVER YOUR PIMPLES. USE A LIGHT HAIR SPRAY.

SHOW UP LATE. BE COOL. WEAR A BEARD OR A MOUSTACHE WEAR SHADES. WEAR PLATFORM SHOES, SO YOU'RE TALLER.

TAKE HER TO PLACES WHERE YOUR FRIENDS CAN SEE YOU. BUT DON'T INTRODUCE HER TO THEM.

TALK ABOUT INTERNATIONAL POLITICAL PROBLEMS, FOREIGN FILMS, ART, MOVIE STAR GOSSIP— DON'T TALK ABOUT PARENTS, SCHOOL, OR SPORTS. TALK ABOUT YOUR FRIENDS WITH CONTEMPT. ALSO, LIE ABOUT YOUR AGE.

DATING YOUR COUSIN

CLASSIC PROBLEMS—

PARENTS

.... BE VERY FIRM.

> NO, MOM!! HE DOES **NOT** WANT CHICKEN SOUP! NO, HE DOES **NOT** WANT A HOT MEAL!! NO, HE DOES **NOT** WANT YOU TO MAKE A SANDWICH TO TAKE TO THE GAME!!

CLASSIC PROBLEM

DATING THE MOST POPULAR BOY

GET A PRINTER TO RUN OFF A FASHION MAGAZINE COVER WITH YOUR PICTURE ON IT... FLASH IT ON THE COMPETITION....

THE PROM

IF YOU CAN'T GET A DATE—SHOW UP ANYHOW... GET AUTOGRAPHS... MAKE NEW FRIENDS, MAKE HISTORY. MAKE EVERYONE FEEL GUILTY.

DATING IDEAS

BE OF HELP IN THE COMMUNITY.

DATING IDEAS